LONDON'S ENVIRO200 BUSES

DAVID BEDDALL

AMBERLEY

I would like to thank my wife Helen for her continuing support whilst writing this book. I would also like to thank Liam Farrer-Beddall for allowing me to use his photographs. Finally, a thank you goes to Jeff Lloyd for allowing me to use his and Colin Lloyd's photographs in this book.

First published 2023

Amberley Publishing
The Hill, Stroud
Gloucestershire, GL5 4EP

www.amberley-books.com

Copyright © David Beddall, 2023

The right of David Beddall to be identified as the Author of this work has been asserted in accordance with the Copyrights, Designs and Patents Act 1988.

ISBN 978 1 3981 0642 0 (print)
ISBN 978 1 3981 0643 7 (ebook)

British Library Cataloguing in Publication Data.
A catalogue record for this book is available from the British Library.

Origination by Amberley Publishing.
Printed in the UK.

Introduction

The Enviro200 was first introduced in 2004 under the Transbus name. The demonstration model featured a dual-door layout – one at the front, one at the back. However, this layout was not popular and the model was redesigned. A second attempt at the model was introduced in 2006, this version being much more successful. The Enviro200 replaced the Dennis Dart SLF chassis, along with the Plaxton Pointer bodywork. The new model proved popular with operators in the UK, and became one of the standard vehicles used for fleet replacement in London. It was available as an integral vehicle, this being the most popular choice. However, the Enviro200 chassis could also be found carrying Optare Esteem or MCV Evolution bodywork. Small numbers of these body styles were purchased for operation in the London area. In early 2007 the Enviro200 body became available on the MAN 14.240 chassis.

The chassis was originally built in Falkirk, but due to volume orders being placed by operators for the Enviro400, Alexander Dennis took the decision in 2007 to move the majority of Enviro200 production to the former Plaxton works in Scarborough.

A hybrid version of the Enviro200, known as the Enviro200H, was introduced in 2008. Five such vehicles were put to use in London service. In 2011 the chassis was relaunched as the AD E20D. The 'classic' Enviro200 ceased production in 2018 in favour of the new MMC model.

The next generation of Enviro200 model was launched in 2014, becoming known as the Enviro200 MMC (Major Model Change). The introduction of this model saw the original Enviro200 design referred to as the 'classic' Enviro200. The MMC model featured a revised look, as will be seen throughout this book. The first of this new type entered service in London during 2015 and a large number now operate in the capital.

2015 also saw the launch of the Enviro200 MMCEV, this being an all-electric version based on the BYD K9 chassis, and later the BYD D8UR variant. There are now over 200 of this type in service in London, with Go-Ahead London boasting over 150 of this model, as of July 2021. Metroline and RATP London also have sizable batches, with Stagecoach London having five in stock.

The aim of this book is to provide a potted history of the Enviro200 model in London up until July 2021.

February 2005 saw the arrival of an Enviro200 demonstrator made by Transbus. It initially operated with London United before moving to Metroline at the end of March. It was used from Holloway on route 214. In May it was again loaned to Metroline after a stint with First London. It is photographed in Islington operating route 274. (Colin Lloyd/Jeff Lloyd Collection)

East London Bus Group took stock of the first batch of Enviro200s in November 2006 for route 273, the route commencing in January 2007. The first of the batch was registered LX56 DZU, and was originally numbered 36001. When Stagecoach repurchased the London operations these were renumbered in the 36300 series. 36001 is seen in Lewisham wearing its new number 36301. (Liam Farrer-Beddall)

Bromley received four more Enviro200s in September 2008 for use on route 246. The penultimate member of this small batch, 36012 (LX58 CAE), is seen attending the Showbus 2008 rally at the Imperial War Museum, Duxford, showing off the Selkent fleet names. (Liam Farrer-Beddall)

Thirteen 8.9-metre-long Enviro200s were taken into stock by the Selkent division of the East London Bus Group in September 2008. They were shared between Catford and Bromley garages for routes 356 and 354. Originally number 36015, LX58 CAV was renumbered 36315 under Stagecoach ownership. It is seen in Bromley operating route 354. (Liam Farrer-Beddall)

Further Enviro200s arrived in October, this time measuring 9.3 metres in length. They were again allocated to Selkent, this time being added to Plumstead's allocation. 36027 (LX58 CCN) is seen loading in Woolwich, operating route 386. (David Beddall)

36342 (LX09 ADO) was new as 36042. It formed part of a batch of seven ADL Enviro200s allocated to Rainham garage for use on route 372. It is seen approaching Lakeside bus station. (Liam Farrer-Beddall)

The largest batch of Enviro200s to be purchased by the East London Bus Group was allocated to East London's West Ham garage for route D3. 36059 (LX59 AOK) is seen passing Canning Town having just departed from West Ham garage to start service on the D3. (Liam Farrer-Beddall)

Route 323 (Canning Town–Mile End) received a batch of four Enviro200s in December 2009, these being allocated to West Ham. Originally numbered 36062–5, the batch became known as 36362–5 under Stagecoach ownership. The first member of the batch, 36362 (LX59 CEF), is seen about to enter Canning Town station having travelled the short distance from West Ham. (Liam Farrer-Beddall)

The final batch of Enviro200s for the East London Bus Group were again allocated to West Ham, this time for route 488. Although intended for route 488, they were used on any of West Ham's single-deck routes. 36374 (LX59 EDL) is seen operating route D3, departing Crossharbour Asda. (Liam Farrer-Beddall)

Arriva London received its first batch of Enviro200s in March 2007. At this time ten 9.3-metre Enviro200s arrived at Clapton for use on route 393. Later in the year the route was extended to Chalk Farm, with four additional Enviro200s arriving. ENS4 (LJ07 EDP) is seen in Hackney, heading towards Chalk Farm. (Liam Farrer-Beddall)

A month later nine longer 10.2-metre Enviro200s were delivered to Croydon for route T31. ENL6 (LJ07 EDF) is seen off route in Croydon, operating route 312 to South Croydon garage. (Liam Farrer-Beddall)

The 2008 deliveries commenced in January with a batch of thirteen EN-class Enviro200s at Lea Valley. They were acquired for use on route 192 between Enfield and Tottenham Hale. EN3 (LJ57 USU) is seen on layover in Enfield blinded for its return journey to Tottenham Hale. (David Beddall)

No further Enviro200s were received by Arriva London until October 2008 when eleven longer 10.2-metre saloons arrived to operate route 491. ENL15 (LJ58 AVZ) is seen departing Waltham Cross bus station bound for North Middlesex Hospital. (Liam Farrer-Beddall)

ENL26 (LJ58 AVC) was one of nine Enviro200s purchased for use on route 166. It is seen heading towards Banstead while passing through Croydon. (Liam Farrer-Beddall)

Eighteen 10.2-metre Enviro200s arrived in May and June 2009 at Wood Green for use on the 184 between Turnpike Lane and Barnet. ENL30 (LJ09 KPR) is photographed having just left Turnpike Lane, the station building seen on the right. (Liam Farrer-Beddall)

Thirteen 10.2-m Enviro200s arrived at Barking for use on the 325 in February 2010, entering service the month after. ENL57 (LJ10 CSY) was one of these vehicles and is seen about to enter East Ham town centre. (Liam Farrer-Beddall)

The next batch of thirteen ENLs were also allocated to Barking, this time for use on the 173. However, they were mixed with the 325 batch, as shown by ENL68 (LJ60 AYM). It is captured by the camera heading towards East Becton Sainsbury's on route 325. (Liam Farrer-Beddall)

Ponders End garage took stock of eight 10.8-metre Enviro200s in October 2011, introducing a fourth class: the ENX. ENX4 (LJ61 CKL) is seen on the 313 at Potters Bar station. (Liam Farrer-Beddall)

Arriva London won the contract for routes 397 and W11 in 2012, with fourteen 9.6-metre Enviro200s acquired. ENS16 (LJ12 BYZ) is seen passing through Walthamstow bus station bound for Chingford Hall Estate. (Liam Farrer-Beddall)

July 2012 saw the arrival of a further eleven 10.8-metre Enviro200s, this time at Thornton Heath. ENX9-19 were purchased for use on route 289. ENX13 (LJ12 BXY) is seen passing its home garage heading towards Elmers End. (Liam Farrer-Beddall)

April 2013 saw the transfer of seven short Enviro200s from Arriva Southern Counties to Arriva London. Allocated to Lea Valley, the batch were used to replace Pointer Darts on route 318. EN18 (GN57 BPO) is photographed passing through Stamford Hill. (Liam Farrer-Beddall)

Former Arriva the Shires 3818 (GN08 CHG) is seen departing Harrow bus station on local route H19. It is seen displaying its new fleet number, ENL89. (Liam Farrer-Beddall)

Romford station finds ENL90 (GN08 CHH), one of many Enviro200s acquired from Arriva Southern Counties. It is seen operating the one-vehicle route 347, which the company won in October 2015. (Liam Farrer-Beddall)

A reorganisation of the Arriva operations in London and the home counties in January 2016 saw the London routes of Arriva the Shires and Arriva Southern Counties transfer to the control of Arriva London. GN08 CHD was new to Arriva Southern Counties as 4007. It gained a new rolling stock number, ENL87, with Arriva London. It is seen entering Bluewater bus station. (Liam Farrer-Beddall)

Arriva London were successful in gaining a number of contracts in the Bexleyheath area. ENX23 (GN09 AVY) was new to Arriva Southern Counties as 4031. It is seen operating route B12, entering Bexleyheath town centre. (Liam Farrer-Beddall)

Arriva Southern Counties won the contract for the B13, commencing on 23 January 2016. For the route seven AD Enviro200 MMCs were purchased. They arrived in January 2016 and were numbered in the Arriva London sequence. ENR4 (LK65 EKT) is seen on layover in Bexleyheath. The batch initially operated on the Arriva Kent Thameside operators' licence. (Liam Farrer-Beddall)

Arriva London inherited a fleet of Wright Cadet-bodied DAF SB120 saloon from Arriva the Shires in January 2016, which proved somewhat troublesome. To help the situation Arriva London purchased twelve Enviro200s, new to Stagecoach London, and allocated them to the SB120 routes. ENL102 (LX11 AWM) is seen departing Edgware bus station on route 303 to Colindale. (Liam Farrer-Beddall)

The next batch of Enviro200 MMCs arrived in June 2016. EN34–8 were allocated to Ponders End for use on route 377. The last of the batch, EN38 (LK16 BYA), is seen passing through Enfield town centre bound for Ponders End. (Liam Farrer-Beddall)

November 2017 saw the arrival of eleven 9.75-metre Enviro200 MMCs for use on route W6. The first of the batch, ENS29 (YX67 VHL), is seen departing Southgate station. (Liam Farrer-Beddall)

ENN39–54 were delivered to Arriva London in November and December 2017 to renew the rolling stock on route W4. They arrived early, the contract not starting until February 2018. ENN43 (YY67 HCF) is seen passing Turnpike Lane on its way to Oakthorpe Park. (Liam Farrer-Beddall)

November also saw the arrival of a pair of longer 10.9-metre Enviro200 MMCs at Thornton Heath, where they were used on the 289. The first of the pair, ENX31 (YX67 VHJ), is seen passing West Croydon bus station bound for Purley. (Liam Farrer-Beddall)

As of July 2021, ENN55–71 is the newest batch of Enviro200 MMCs to be purchased by Arriva London. They arrived in October 2019 at Ponders End for use on the 192. ENN68 (YX69 NYR) is seen entering Edmonton Green bus station on its way to Enfield. The new Arriva logo can be seen on the vehicle. (Liam Farrer-Beddall)

Go-Ahead London received their first Enviro200s in March 2007. At this time seventeen were purchased for use on route 200. SE1 (LX07 BXH) is seen operating the route passing through Wimbledon. (Liam Farrer-Beddall)

Eleven MCV Evolution-bodied Enviro200s replaced a similar number of Caetano Nimbus-bodied Transbus Dart saloons on route 167. ED18–28 arrived in May and initially wore Docklands Buses fleet names as demonstrated by ED20 (LX07 BYL). It is seen leaving Ilford for Debden. (Liam Farrer-Beddall)

Delivery of the next batch of Enviro200s were spread between June and October 2007. SE18–35 were allocated to the newly acquired Blue Triangle business for route 364. The first three were delivered to Blue Triangle under their ownership. The last of the batch, SE35 (SN57 DXB), is photographed at Ilford Broadway. (David Beddall)

The 2009 delivery of Enviro200s were bodied by East Lancs with the Esteem model. Forty of the type were shared between Merton (routes 163 and 164) and Sutton (route 80). SOE1 (LX09 AYF) was one of those allocated to Merton. It is photographed parked in Wimbledon town centre. (Liam Farrer-Beddall)

A few years passed before the next Enviro200s entered the Go-Ahead London fleet. A small batch were delivered to Silvertown garage in February and March 2010 for use on the 300. SE38 (LX10 AUR) is seen at Canning Town bound for East Ham. (Liam Farrer-Beddall)

Stockwell received its first batch of Enviro200s in November 2010 when eight were taken into stock for use on route 170. SE51 (YX60 EOJ) is seen on layover at Victoria before returning to Roehampton. (Liam Farrer-Beddall)

December 2010 saw the arrival of thirty Enviro200s with London Central in south-east London. The batch was split between Bexleyheath and Belvedere garages from where they operated routes 244, B11 and B16. SE66 (YX60 EOP) is seen operating route B16, entering Bexleyheath town centre. (Liam Farrer-Beddall)

The next nine Enviro200s arrived in April 2011. They were allocated to Camberwell for use on route P5. SE87 (YX11 CPK) is seen approaching journey's end at Elephant & Castle. (Liam Farrer-Beddall)

A second batch of Enviro200s were allocated to the Blue Triangle operation in the summer of 2011. SE94–103 were allocated to route 376 from Rainham. SE96 (SN11 FGC) is seen heading towards Beckton station at East Ham. (Liam Farrer-Beddall)

Docklands Buses took stock of thirty-eight Enviro200s in August and September 2011. They were shared between routes 276 and D6, and were allocated to Silvertown. SE111 (YX61 BYG) is seen operating route D6, loading at Crossharbour Asda. (Liam Farrer-Beddall)

At Stratford bus station we find a rather dirty SE136 (YX61 BWM), another of the thirty-eight-strong batch of Enviro200s delivered to Go-Ahead London's Docklands Buses division in the summer of 2011. It is seen heading towards Newham Hospital on route 276. (Liam Farrer-Beddall)

Docklands Buses also received eleven additional Enviro200s in September 2011 for use on the D8. The penultimate member of the batch, SE151 (YX61 DTY), is seen on layover at Crossharbour. (Liam Farrer-Beddall)

September 2011 was a busy month for the intake of Enviro200s by Go-Ahead London. In addition to those already mentioned that were taken into stock by Docklands Buses, an additional fourteen Enviro200s were received by London Central. SE153–166 were allocated to Peckham for use on the P12. SE161 (YX61 DVL) is seen loading in Peckham town centre bound for Honor Oak Park. (Liam Farrer-Beddall)

Eight Enviro200s followed in November 2011 and were allocated to Sutton for route 413. SE171 (YX61 EKK) is seen at Morden off route, operating the 80. (Liam Farrer-Beddall)

The only new Enviro200s to arrive in 2012 were allocated to Plough Lane for use on the 493. SE179 (SN12 AUT) is seen in a wet Richmond. (Liam Farrer-Beddall)

First London's Northumberland Park garage was purchased by Go-Ahead London in March 2012. This brought twenty-nine Enviro200s into the Go-Ahead fleet, which gained classification code SEN. SEN18 (YX11 FYY) was one of those acquired, and is seen in Muswell Hill. (David Beddall)

Go-Ahead London were successful in winning the tender for route 286 from Arriva Southern Counties in July 2014. For this, fifteen Enviro200s were taken into stock by London Central at New Cross. SE210 (YY14 WEO) is seen passing through Eltham heading for the Greenwich terminus, which is located close to the Cutty Sark. (Liam Farrer-Beddall)

Route 100 was the next service to receive a batch of Enviro200s. Nineteen SEs were purchased for the route, all of which were allocated to Mandela Way garage. SE228 (YY64 TXN) is seen paused at traffic lights before crossing Bishopsgate. (Liam Farrer-Beddall)

April 2015 saw the arrival of twenty-six Enviro200s at Plough Lane for use on routes 322 and G1. SE248 (YY15 EYV) is seen at Clapham Junction operating route G1 to Battersea. (Liam Farrer-Beddall)

From 1 July 2014 the London operations of Metrobus came under the control of Go-Ahead London, retaining the Metrobus fleet name. A large number of Enviro200s were acquired in the process, which will be shown later in the book. In October 2015 seven Enviro200s were allocated to Metrobus for use on route 352. SE262 (YX65 RJY) is captured by the camera passing through a wet Bromley. (Liam Farrer-Beddall)

November 2015 saw the arrival of twenty Enviro200s to cover an increase in the PVR on route 80, along with the contract renewal of the 164. The last of the batch, SE287 (YX65 RTO), is seen passing through Tooting Broadway off-route, on the 219 to Wimbledon. (Liam Farrer-Beddall)

The last three 'classic' Enviro200s to be purchased by Go-Ahead London were added to the Metrobus operation, topping up the requirement on route 162. The first of the trio was SE288 (SN16 OLP), which is seen in Eltham town centre. (Liam Farrer-Beddall)

Compared with other London operators, Go-Ahead London was late in taking stock of the Enviro200 MMC model. The first two arrived in April 2016 at Camberwell, where they were used to cover an increase on the P5. SE292 (YX16 OCY) is seen in Brixton operating the P5 to Patmore Estate. (Liam Farrer-Beddall)

A third variant of the Enviro200 was introduced in 2015, with the first fifty-one Enviro200 MMCEVs entering service from Waterloo garage in 2016 on routes 507 and 521. These were the first all-electric singles to operate in London and were based on the BYD D9UR chassis. SEe4 (LJ16 NNH) is seen at Waterloo having just started its journey to London Bridge via the City of London. (Liam Farrer-Beddall)

Further BYDs arrived in November 2017, this time to replace the WHY-class Wrightbus Electrocity saloons on the 360. SEe52–65 were allocated to Camberwell for use on the service. SEe58 (LJ67 DJV) is seen at Elephant & Castle. (Liam Farrer-Beddall)

Route 153 was taken over in January 2018 from CT Plus, bringing with it another eleven BYD/ Enviro200 MMCEV saloons. By this time the chassis had changed to the D8UR model. SEe68 (LJ67 DKU) is seen heading towards Finsbury Park, passing through Holloway Road. (Liam Farrer-Beddall)

The single-deck routes that passed through the Kings Cross/St Pancras areas were converted to all-electric single-decks. Go-Ahead London won the contract for the 214 from Metroline, commencing in August 2019. Kings Cross provides the backdrop of this photograph of SEe91 (LA19 KAX), seen heading towards Highgate Village. (Liam Farrer-Beddall)

SE297 (YW19 VSM) was one of eleven Enviro200 MMCs delivered to Go-Ahead London in August 2019 for use on route 209, which at that time was curtailed to Castlenau as a result of the closure of Hammersmith Bridge, and new route 378. SE297 is seen passing through Barnes on its way to Mortlake. (Liam Farrer-Beddall)

River Road, Barking, received a batch of sixteen Enviro200 MMCs for use on route 364 between Dagenham East and Ilford. Delivery was spread over October and November 2019. SE316 (YX69 NNY) is seen passing through Ilford town centre after starting its journey to Dagenham. (Liam Farrer-Beddall)

Another central London route to go all-electric was the 100, doing so in January 2020. For this, eleven Enviro200 MMCEV saloons were taken into stock at Camberwell. SEe101 (LF69 UZC) is seen at Aldgate before completing its journey to St Paul's. The Covid-19 pandemic saw the capacity on buses severely reduced during 2020. This batch could only carry eleven passengers, as shown by the notice on the entrance doors. (Liam Farrer-Beddall)

Further BYD/Enviro200 MMCEV saloons arrived in March 2020, this time for the takeover of the 444 from Tower Transit. Thirteen of the type were purchased and allocated to Northumberland Park. SEe119 (LF20 XNB) is seen on diversion in Wood Green completing the short journey to Turnpike Lane station. (Liam Farrer-Beddall)

The Covid-19 pandemic saw the need for additional buses in London to safely transport school children from September 2020. For this a number of buses were both drafted in from other operators, along with existing rolling stock being reinstated. Go-Ahead London took stock of a small batch of former Abellio London Enviro200 MMCs. SEN52 (YX16 OAG) was one of these, photographed at St Pancras International. (Liam Farrer-Beddall)

Route 184 was another tender win for Go-Ahead London in North London, this time at the expense of Arriva London. SEe129 (LF70 YWH) is seen passing Turnpike Lane station. (Liam Farrer-Beddall)

As of July 2021, route 484 in south-east London was home to the newest batch of Enviro200s in London. SEe146 (LG21 JBU) is seen passing Lewisham police station bound for Camberwell Green. Go-Ahead London was successful in winning the tender for the 484 from Abellio London. (Liam Farrer-Beddall)

NCP Challenger of Twickenham took stock of thirty-six 10.2-metre Enviro200s, with all but one arriving in 2007. ADL15 (SK07 DXW) represents the batch, and is seen passing through Wimbledon on route 493. (David Beddall)

Seven shorter 8.9-metre Enviro200s were also taken into stock during 2007 for use on route E11. ADS04 (SK07 HLP) is seen on layover at Greenford Broadway. (David Beddall)

June 2007 saw the arrival of eleven 8.9-metre Enviro200s at Perivale for route E6. A year later the batch moved across to Potters Bar for various routes. DES794 (LK07 BDX) is seen operating route 383, one of a number of Metroline routes that travel through Barnet town centre. (Liam Farrer-Beddall)

The next batch of Enviro200s to arrive with Metroline were allocated to Potters Bar. Eleven 10.8-metre saloons were put to use on non-Transport for London (TfL) services 84 and 242. DEL854 (LK08 DWG) is captured by the camera on St Peters Street, St Albans, having completed a journey on the 84 from New Barnet. (Liam Farrer-Beddall)

August 2008 saw the first of twenty-eight Enviro200s delivered to Metroline to convert routes 326, C11 and E6. DE867 (LK08 DXA) is seen in Hampstead whilst operating the C11, heading towards Brent Cross. (Liam Farrer-Beddall)

Route 326 received its full complement of Enviro200s in December 2008 when nine of the type entered the Metroline fleet. DE953 (LK58 CSY) was the second member of the batch, and is seen exiting Brent Cross bus station. (Liam Farrer-Beddall)

Like Go-Ahead London, Metroline also received a small batch MCV Evolution-bodied Enviro200 saloons. DM961–70 were purchased for use on the 190 between Richmond and West Brompton, entering the fleet early in 2009. DM962 (LK09 EKJ) is photographed in Richmond, setting off for its journey to West Brompton. (Liam Farrer-Beddall)

The summer of 2009 saw twenty-two Enviro200s arrive with Metroline. These were shared between Brentford, Perivale and Cricklewood. Those at Brentford were put to use on the E8, as shown by DE993 (LK09 ENC). It is photographed at Ealing Broadway. (Liam Farrer-Beddall)

Cricklewood received the next nineteen Enviro200s in October and November 2009, being mostly used on the 316. DE1027 (LK59 AVP) is seen paused at Shepherds Bush station before reaching journey's end at the nearby White City bus station. (Liam Farrer-Beddall)

The 2010 Enviro200 deliveries were all allocated to Cricklewood garage. The first fifteen arrived in June for use on the 143. DE1128 (LK10 BYU) is seen loading at Archway while operating this route towards Brent Cross. (Liam Farrer-Beddall)

July and August 2010 saw the next twenty-two Enviro200s arrive at Cricklewood, this time to convert route C11 to the type. DE1147 (LK10 BZP) is seen about to enter Brent Cross bus station at the end of its journey on the C11 from Archway. (Liam Farrer-Beddall)

Kings Cross received the first Enviro200 deliveries of 2011. Nineteen were delivered over the summer months for use on route 274. DE1163 (LK11 CWY) is seen passing through Marble Arch, destined for Lancaster Gate. (Liam Farrer-Beddall)

Nineteen Enviro200s were ordered for the renewal of rolling stock on the 46. Although they arrived in May and June 2012, they did not see service on their intended route until September. Instead, they were stored and put to use on London 2012 Olympic Games duties over the summer. DE1320 (LK12 AWY) is seen approaching the Eaton Manor Transport Hub. (Liam Farrer-Beddall)

August 2012 saw the introduction of another new class of Enviro200 with Metroline, with delivery being completed in October. By this time twenty-three were being used by Potters Bar on routes 234 and W9. DEM1343 (LK62 DDU) is seen in Muswell Hill operating route 234. (David Beddall)

22 June 2013 saw Metroline acquire some of the west London operations of First London, bringing 213 additional Enviro200s into the fleet. DE1630 (YX58 FPO) represents this big intake, seen at the Central Middlesex Hospital. (Liam Farrer-Beddall)

September 2014 saw the arrival of ten Enviro200s for the 112, allocated to Cricklewood garage. DEL2068 (LK64 ECW) is seen leaving Brent Cross bus station for Ealing Broadway. (Liam Farrer-Beddall)

The first new single-deck rolling stock for a former First London garage arrived in August and September 2015. At this time ten Enviro200s were delivered to Uxbridge. DEL2146 (LK65 EAC) is seen about to enter Uxbridge station having completed a journey on the 331. (Liam Farrer-Beddall)

Twelve 10.9-metre Enviro200 MMCs arrived at Uxbridge in June 2016. They were put to use on the U3, with DEL2159 (LK16 DDU) seen on this service. It is photographed at Heathrow Airport, shortly before it enters the tunnel to the central area of the airport. (Liam Farrer-Beddall)

Brentford received twenty-two Enviro200 MMC saloons in December 2016 for use on the 235. At The Bell, Hounslow, we find DEL2261 (LK66 FTA) heading towards Brentford. (Liam Farrer-Beddall)

Twenty-three BYD/Enviro200 MMC EV saloons entered the Metroline fleet in May and June 2018, purchased to convert route 46 to all-electric rolling stock. However, the introduction of this batch into service did not go smoothly, with problems being encountered with the installation of charging points at Holloway garage. They eventually entered service in October. BEL2523 (LJ18 FHW) is seen passing Kings Cross bound for Lancaster Gate on the 46. (Liam Farrer-Beddall)

Metroline won the contract for the 393 from Arriva London in 2019. For the route, sixteen 9.75-metre Enviro200 MMCs were ordered. However, the vehicles delivered measured 10.9 metres in length, rendering them too long for the 393. Therefore, they were placed into store until a suitable route could be found for them. It was not until the spring of 2020 that these vehicles entered service. They were allocated to Cricklewood for use on the 316 and 112. DEL2611 (YX19 OVP) is seen at Brent Cross operating the 112. (Liam Farrer-Beddall)

The delivery of the longer DELs mentioned in the last caption led to the loan of eight of the ENS class Enviro200s used by Arriva London on the 393. ENS8 (LJ07 EDX) is seen travelling through Holloway bound for Chalk Farm. For the duration of their stay, Metroline fleet names and Holloway garage codes were applied to the vehicles. (Liam Farrer-Beddall)

New rolling stock for the 393 eventually arrived in October 2019, when sixteen shorter 9.7-metre Enviro200 MMCs arrived at Holloway. Their arrival allowed the hired ENS class to return to Arriva London. DEM2690 (YX69 NYV) is seen on Holloway Road heading towards Chalk Farm. (Liam Farrer-Beddall)

The first Enviro200s to enter service on London area routes with Arriva Southern Counties did so in the summer of 2007. A batch of fifteen Enviro200s were used on route 286, displacing older rolling stock. 3987 (GN07 DLU) is photographed in Eltham town centre heading towards Greenwich. (Liam Farrer-Beddall)

Between December 2007 and March 2008 Arriva Southern Counties Grays garage took stock of thirteen Enviro200s for routes 499 and 370. Although delivered as two separate batches, the vehicles could be found interworking the two services. 4000 (GN08 CGO) was one new for route 370, but is seen passing Romford station on route 499. (Liam Farrer-Beddall)

Two batches of Enviro200s were allocated to Dartford in 2008 and 2009 respectively. The 2008 deliveries were shorter Enviro200s for the 233 (Eltham–Swanley). Those delivered to the company in 2009 arrived in January, measuring 10.2 metres. They were primarily purchased for use on the B15, but could also be found on other routes. 4024 (GN58 BUU) is seen in Eltham operating route 126. (Liam Farrer-Beddall)

The final new 'classic' Enviro200s to arrive with Arriva Southern Counties put in an appearance in July and August 2010. They were allocated to Grays garage for use on the 66 between Romford and Leytonstone. The latter location finds 4073 (GN10 KWK), seen on layover before heading back to Romford. (Liam Farrer-Beddall)

A small batch of six East Lancs Esteem-bodied ADL Enviro200 saloons were purchased by CT Plus for use on the W13 between Leytonstone and Woodford Wells. DE3 (PN07 KRD) is seen at the Leytonstone terminus blinded for its return trip. (Liam Farrer-Beddall)

The first two Enviro200s arrived with Hackney Community Transport (CT Plus) in September 2007 to cover an increase on route 394. DAS2 (SN57 DWF) is seen in Islington, heading towards Homerton Hospital. (Liam Farrer-Beddall)

CT Plus took stock of a 10.8-metre single-door Enviro200 in 2010 to operate tours of the Olympic Park in Stratford, connecting with the nearby Stratford rail station. For this, a special pink livery was applied to the vehicle, as seen in the photograph above. DA1 (MX10 DXR) is seen passing the back end of the Olympic Park. (Liam Farrer-Beddall)

CT Plus renewed the rolling stock on the 153 (Liverpool Street–Finsbury Park) upon the re-award of the contract to the company in 2012. DA3 (YX62 DHD) is seen heading towards Central London at Finsbury Park. (Liam Farrer-Beddall)

Seventeen new classic Enviro200s were delivered in 2016 alongside a couple of batches of Enviro200 MMCs. 1221–1237 were put to use on the W19. 1228 (YX66 WGA) is seen at Ilford Broadway. (Liam Farrer-Beddall)

February 2017 saw the arrival of twenty-two Enviro200 MMC saloons for routes W11 and W16, with an extra for route 309. These vehicles were garaged at the newly opened Walthamstow Stadium facility. However, the Enviro200s also got used on other services. 1249 (YY66 PYU) is seen exiting Walthamstow bus station, continuing its journey on the W19 to Ilford. (Liam Farrer-Beddall)

Seven longer 10.9-metre Enviro200 MMCs replaced the East Lancs Esteem-bodied ADL Enviro200 saloons on route W13 in February 2017. 1266 (YX17 NWG) is seen at Leytonstone while operating this service. (Liam Farrer-Beddall)

Eleven short Enviro200 MMCs replaced the DCS class Caetano Slimbus-bodied Dart SLFs on the 394 in March 2017. 1273 (YX17 NWT) is seen on layover at the Homerton Hospital terminus. (Liam Farrer-Beddall)

CT Plus gained the contract for the D6 from Go-Ahead London in September 2018, for which thirteen Enviro200 MMCs were purchased, which arrived in August. 1288 (YX68 UJF) is seen heading towards Ash Grove, passing through Mile End. (Liam Farrer-Beddall)

Additional single-decks were needed by CT Plus in 2019 to cover an increase on routes W11 and W19. Five classic Enviro200s were sourced, originating with First London. The first of the five, 1336 (YX11 AFE), is seen in Ilford on route W19. (Liam Farrer-Beddall)

The first batch of six Enviro200s received by First London were intended for route 498. However, the deferral of the start date for this service saw the batch initially allocated to Uxbridge instead of Dagenham. The 498 started in June 2008, with the fleet moving across to Dagenham at this time. DML44005 (LK57 EJJ) is seen at Romford station operating route 165. (Liam Farrer-Beddall)

Uxbridge received their intended batch in the summer of 2008, when fifteen Enviro200s were taken into stock for routes A10, U10 and 331. DML44009 (LK08 FNH) is seen departing Uxbridge station bound for Ruislip on the U10. (Liam Farrer-Beddall)

The Enviro200 grew in popularity with First, with eighty-six 10.2-metre DML class examples being ordered by the company for 2008/early 2009 delivery. The first twenty-two went to Alperton for use on the 245. DML44024 (YX58 DUJ) is seen at Golders Green before departing for Alperton Sainsbury's. (Liam Farrer-Beddall)

Twenty-seven DMLs arrived at Willesden Junction between December 2008 and February 2009 for conversion of routes 226 and 228 to the type. DML44055 (YX58 FPT) was one of this batch and is seen in Harlesden operating route 228 to Maida Vale. (Liam Farrer-Beddall)

February 2009 also saw the arrival of twelve Enviro200s at Dagenham for use on route 165. DML44073 (YX58 HVC) is seen passing Romford station while heading towards The Brewery, Romford, on route 165. (Liam Farrer-Beddall)

The final batch of the eighty-six-strong order were allocated to Willesden Junction for routes 187 and 487. DML44089 (YX09 AEG) is seen paused in Harlesden while operating route 187. (Liam Farrer-Beddall)

Investment was made in new rolling stock for the Greenford and Ealing area services in 2009, with new Enviro200s arriving over the summer months. Twenty shorter 8.9-metre Enviro200s arrived between May and July, which were given the DMS classification code. They were put to use on routes E5 and E10. DMS44403 (YX09 FMD) is seen operating route E5, photographed in Greenford. (Liam Farrer-Beddall)

June and July saw another batch of twenty DML class Enviro200s enter service at Greenford for routes E7 and E9. Another fifteen arrived at Greenford in March 2010 for use on route 195, a route won by First London from Ealing Community Transport. DML44136 is (YX10 BDU) captured by the camera in Brentford before returning to the Charville Lane Estate. (Liam Farrer-Beddall)

April 2010 deliveries were allocated to Uxbridge to update the rolling stock from this garage, with two additional Enviro200s arriving at the same garage in September. DML44157 (YX10 BFZ) is seen departing Uxbridge station on route U5 to Hayes and Harlington. (Liam Farrer-Beddall)

January 2011 saw the arrival of twelve shorter 8.9-metre Enviro200s at Northumberland Park for use on the W4. DMS44423 (YX60 FUD) is captured passing through Wood Green. (Liam Farrer-Beddall)

2011 also saw the arrival of twenty-three DML class Enviro200s. DML44171–93 were shared between Dagenham (for route 368) and Greenford (for the 95), all arriving in stock by April. DML44172 (YX11 AFN) was one of those allocated to Dagenham. It is seen loading in Barking town centre on its way to Chadwell Heath. (Liam Farrer-Beddall)

A third set of Enviro200 was introduced to the First London fleet in the summer of 2011. The 9.3-metre saloon was given classification code DM. The first members of the type were allocated to Northumberland Park for use on the 299, with seven more being allocated to Alperton. February 2012 saw more DM class Enviro200s arrive. DM44260–70 were allocated to Lea Interchange for the W14, while DM44293–301 were allocated to Northumberland Park for the W16. DM44207 (YX61 EKY) was one of those allocated to Alperton and is seen in Wembley on route 223. (Liam Farrer-Beddall)

A fourth set of Enviro200s arrived in February 2012, measuring 10.8 metres. These were classified as DMV. Nine arrived at Lea Interchange for route 308, while Dagenham took stock of eight for route 368. Dagenham-based DMV44274 (YX61 FZS) is seen passing through Barking en route to Chadwell Heath. (Liam Farrer-Beddall)

March and April 2012 saw two further batch of DMVs arrive with First London. The first sixteen (DMV44221–36) were allocated to Lea Interchange for route 236. The second were put to use on the 206 from Willesden Junction. DMV44225 (YX12 AEW) is photographed at Finsbury Park while operating route 236. (Liam Farrer-Beddall)

DML44279–92 were allocated to Lea Interchange in February 2012 for route W15. The first of the batch, DML44279 (YX61 FYB), is seen passing the Olympic Park in 2012. (Liam Farrer-Beddall)

The final Enviro200s to enter the First London fleet arrived in May and June 2012, both batches comprising 10.2-metre examples. DML44209–20 were allocated to Alperton for the 224, while DML44313–28 arrived at Westbourne Park for use on the 70. DML44321 (YX12 ARZ) is seen heading towards South Kensington on route 70 when photographed at Notting Hill Gate. (Liam Farrer-Beddall)

February 2007 saw the first Enviro200 saloons enter the Quality Line fleet. Like other operators already shown, the initial batch carried other bodywork, in this case the East Lancs Esteem. Fleet numbers SD43–51 were allocated to the batch, which were put to use on route S1. Seen in Sutton town centre, SD44 (PE56 UFJ) is heading towards Mitcham on the S1. SD52 and SD53 were delivered the following month. (Liam Farrer-Beddall)

The first 'classic' Enviro200 arrived with Quality Line in January 2008 to cover an extension of route S3. Almost seven years later, in December 2014, a batch of six Enviro200s were taken into stock to upgrade the rolling stock on the S3. The first of this batch, SD55 (YY64 TXB), is seen entering Sutton town centre. (Liam Farrer-Beddall)

July 2008 saw the first Enviro200s enter the London United/London Sovereign fleet. Ten short 8.9-metre saloons were allocated to Tolworth for use on Kingston area service K1, replacing Pointer MPD-bodied Dart SLFs. SDE6 (YX08 MEU) is seen exiting Kingston's Cromwell Road bus station on its outward journey to New Malden station. (Liam Farrer-Beddall)

August 2008 saw a second batch of Enviro200s arrive with London United, this time measuring 10.2 metres. They were allocated the DE class code and were used on the 285 from Hounslow Heath. DE1 (YX58 DVA) is seen alighting passengers in Kingston town centre. (Liam Farrer-Beddall)

Originally intended for East Thames Buses, five hybrid Enviro200s were taken into stock by London United at Fulwell in April 2009 and used on route 371. Numbered HDE1–5, these vehicles looked smart in the green leaf livery. HDE1 (SN09 CHC) is seen wearing this livery when photographed in Kingston. (Liam Farrer-Beddall)

July 2009 saw the arrival of twenty-eight DE class Enviro200s, which were split between Fulwell (for the 371) and Shepherds Bush (for the 72). DE40 (YX09 HKJ) was one of those allocated to Shepherds Bush for the 72. It is seen rounding Shepherds Bush Green heading towards East Acton. (Liam Farrer-Beddall)

London Sovereign took stock of seven DE class saloons in August 2009 for use in the Northolt area. DE54 (YX59 BYF) is seen after the London Sovereign operation was purchased by the RATP Group. It is seen loading at Harrow bus station operating local route H14 to Hatch End. (Liam Farrer-Beddall)

2010 saw the delivery of thirty-six Enviro200s. The first sixteen arrived in May and were allocated to the former NCP Challenger garage at Park Royal. The second batch of twenty arrived in October and were allocated to Fulwell for route 33. DE114 (YX60 CBF) was part of this latter batch and is seen at Richmond bus station operating the 33 to Fulwell. (Liam Farrer-Beddall)

A second batch of 8.9-metre SDE class Enviro200s entered the London Sovereign fleet in October 2010. They were allocated to Edgware from where they were used on the 324. SDE19 (YX60 BZB) is seen loading at Brent Cross bus station before completing the short journey to nearby Brent Cross Tesco. (Liam Farrer-Beddall)

Twenty-five 10.8-metre Enviro200s were delivered to London United between January and April 2011. The batch were allocated to Hounslow for use on routes H98 and 423. DLE5 (SN60 EBD) is seen parked at Hounslow bus station before heading to Hayes End on route H98. (Liam Farrer-Beddall)

The first Enviro200 MMCs arrived with London United in June 2016. Originally numbered DE28001–14, they took fleet numbers DE20129–42 before entering service from Fulwell on the 265. May 2017 saw the batch renumbered again to DLE30027–40. DE20129 (LJ16 EXL) is seen at the Putney Bridge terminus of route 265. (Liam Farrer-Beddall)

2017 saw the next batch of Enviro200s taken into stock. DLE30041–8 arrived at Hounslow Heath for route 110. DLE30049–70 were allocated to Shepherds Bush, with the exception of DLE30070, which was allocated to Epsom. The main batch were used as a temporary fleet on route 70 before the arrival of the all-electric BE class saloons. DLE30054 (SN17 MVA) is seen departing the Ladbrooke Grove Sainsbury's stop. (Liam Farrer-Beddall)

The shorter midibus requirements were taken care of by three batches of shorter Enviro200 MMCs. In July 2018 a batch of five 9-metre saloons arrived for use on the K4 from Tolworth. Two years later, in August 2020, thirteen similar length Enviro200 MMCs arrived at the same garage for the K1. Both batches were preceded by eight 9.75-metre Enviro200 MMCs at Epsom. They entered the fleet in January 2018, replacing Optare Solo SRs on route 470. SDE20293 (YY67 UUM) represents the batch, photographed in Sutton. (Liam Farrer-Beddall)

2018 and 2019 saw heavy investment by the RATP Group in new Enviro200 MMC saloons for London United, displacing the large fleet of Dart SLF saloons. A start was made on this in 2018 with the introduction of thirty-three 10.9-metre Enviro200s on Kingston area services 216, K2, K3 and K4. DLE30239 (SN18 KPY) represents this large batch of saloons, seen operating route K3 in Kingston. (Liam Farrer-Beddall)

Investment continued with eighty-one DLE class saloons being delivered between August 2018 and January 2019. These were split between Harrow, Edgware, Stamford Brook and Atlas Road garages for various routes. DLE30315 (YX68 URW) represents this large batch of saloons. It is photographed passing through Shepherd's Bush on route 283 to East Acton. (Liam Farrer-Beddall)

Twenty 11.5-metre Enviro200 MMCs arrived with the RATP Group between September 2018 and April 2019. Seven were allocated to Epsom for use on route 293. The other thirteen were allocated to Hounslow for use on the H37, replacing Optare Tempos. DXE30354 (YX19 OLJ) formed part of the latter batch and is seen in Hounslow heading towards Richmond. (Liam Farrer-Beddall)

May 2019 saw twenty-one 10.5-metre Enviro200 MMC saloons enter the London United fleet, introducing the DME class. DME30361–72 were allocated to Atlas Road for use on the 440, with DME30373–81 being allocated to Stamford Brook for route 272. DME30372 (YX19 OMJ) is seen passing a 'classic' Enviro200 at the Central Middlesex Hospital while operating the 440. (Liam Farrer-Beddall)

Thirty-six BYD D8UR saloons, complete with AD Enviro200 MMCEV bodywork, were delivered to London United between June and September 2018. They displaced Enviro200 MMCs on routes 70 and C1. The batch were allocated to Shepherds Bush garage. BE37012 (LJ18 FJP) is seen on route 70 at Ladbrooke Grove Sainsbury's. (Liam Farrer-Beddall)

NED Railways purchased the Travel London operation in 2009, with the company being renamed Abellio London on 30 October. Twenty-four Enviro200s were acquired with the operation, dating between 2006 and 2008. 8507 (LJ08 CZP) is seen paused at Richmond bus station on its way to Heathrow Terminal 5. (Liam Farrer-Beddall)

Thirty-six 10.2-metre Enviro200s were delivered to Abellio London between October 2009 and June 2010. Thirteen were allocated to Beddington in October 2009 for route 407. The others arrived in May and June 2010 at Fulwell for routes R68 and R70. 8532 (YX10 FEJ) is seen at Richmond operating route R68. (Liam Farrer-Beddall)

Thirteen Enviro200s entered the Abellio London fleet in February and March 2011. They were allocated to Walworth garage, being put to use on the 484. 8330 (YX11 AHA) is seen at Camberwell Green, travelling to Lewisham. (Liam Farrer-Beddall)

Thirty-one 10.2-metre Enviro200s were taken into stock by Abellio London between February 2011 and February 2012. 8577 (YX61 GAA) was the one delivered in February 2012, being allocated to Fulwell. It is photographed at Staines before heading back to Twickenham on route 290. (Liam Farrer-Beddall)

Longer 10.8-metre Enviro200s arrived between November 2011 and July 2012, being allocated to both Fulwell and Beddington garages for routes 152, 290 and 490. 8790 (YX12 GHD) was delivered in July 2012 for route 490. It is seen leaving Twickenham town centre for Heathrow Terminal 5. (Liam Farrer-Beddall)

June 2013 saw Kingston area services K1 and K3 gain new rolling stock. The K1 took stock of 8118–27, measuring 8.9 metres. The K3 gained a batch of 10.8-metre Enviro200s numbered 8806–17. 8121 (YX13 EHH) is seen departing Cromwell Road bus station, Kingston. (Liam Farrer-Beddall)

Twenty-seven Enviro200s entered service from Beddington between November 2014 and January 2015. They were put to use on routes S4, 201 and 407. Those on the S4 were numbered 8201–7 and measured 8.9 metres, while the other examples were 10.8-metre buses numbered 8820–43. 8831 (YY64 YJN) is seen passing Arriva London's Brixton garage operating route 201 to Herne Hill. (Liam Farrer-Beddall)

A large number of 10.9-metre Enviro200 MMCs entered the Abellio London fleet between February 2016 and May 2017. 8844–64 were first to arrive, being allocated to Walworth for route C10. In May 2016, 8865–76 arrived at Hayes for route E7. The final batch arrived in April and May 2017 for routes 195 and U5. 8852 (YX16 OAB) is seen departing Canada Water bus station on route C10 towards Victoria. (Liam Farrer-Beddall)

Abellio London were awarded the contract for the 367 in 2016 and placed an order for ten 9-metre Enviro200 MMCs. 8210–9 were allocated to Beddington garage for use on the service. 8214 (YX1 6OBC) is seen heading towards Bromley North as it passes through Bromley town centre. (Liam Farrer-Beddall)

Between April 2016 and August 2017 Abellio took stock of a number of 8.9-metre and 9-metre Enviro200 MMCs, these taking up rolling stock numbers 8138 to 8184. They were shared between Fulwell, Hayes and Beddington garages for various small-bus contracts. 8185 to 8196 arrived in August 2017 and measured 10.9 metres. 8153 (YX16 OFA) formed part of a batch allocated to Fulwell for route E5. It is photographed in Greenford Broadway. (Liam Farrer-Beddall)

Slightly shorter Enviro200 MMCs 8220–31 arrived in September 2017 for route R70. 8232–46 arrived in May and June 2019, this batch being used on the E10 and E11. Both batches measured 10.5 metres in length. 8233 (YX19 OPN) is seen rounding Ealing Broadway having just completed a journey on the E10. (Liam Farrer-Beddall)

708 (YX58 DXD) was one of only three ADL Enviro200s to be fitted to the MAN 18.310 chassis in London. They were purchased for use on route T32 in south London. It is photographed on layover at New Addington. (Liam Farrer-Beddall)

Metrobus acquired the Horsham operations of Arriva Southern Counties on 3 October 2009. Six Enviro200s were included in this sale, which were used on London route 465. The first of the batch was 220 (GN07 AVR), and is seen approaching Cromwell Road bus station in Kingston. (Liam Farrer-Beddall)

The majority of Enviro200s delivered to Metrobus measured 8.9 metres and were allocated to Green Street Green. Although they were purchased for specific routes, they were often found on the majority of single-deck routes from that garage. This is exemplified by 149 (YX60 FTP), new in January 2011 for route B14, on route 162 at Bromley. The first two months of 2011 saw the arrival of two batches numbered 148 to 162. (Liam Farrer-Beddall)

Orpington area route R9 required a batch of longer single-decks. Three 10.2-metre Enviro200s were purchased by Metrobus in July 2011 and allocated to Green Street Green. 731 (YX11 CTE) was the first of the trio. (Liam Farrer-Beddall)

November 2011 saw the arrival of sixteen shorter Enviro200s for routes R1 and R11. 166 (YX61 ENH) is seen about to enter Orpington town centre heading towards Queen Mary Hospital on route R11. (Liam Farrer-Beddall)

Ten 8.9-metre Enviro200s arrived at Green Street Green in February and March 2013 for routes 233 and 138. The first of the batch, 179 (YX62 DYH), is seen in Eltham town centre on route 233. (Liam Farrer-Beddall)

The final batch of Enviro200s taken into stock by Metrobus for London area services were thirteen longer saloons for the 284. 751 (YX13 AGV) is seen heading towards Grove Park Cemetery on the 284. It was new to the company in March 2013. (Liam Farrer-Beddall)

Stagecoach re-entered the London bus scene in October 2010, reacquiring the East London and Selkent operations. A number of Enviro200s had been purchased by the East London Bus Group, which were taken into stock by Stagecoach. Photographs of these can be seen at the beginning of the book. 2011 saw further fleet replacement with a number of Enviro200s entering the fleet. Seven were allocated to North Street, Romford, in March for route 296. 36265 (LX11 AVV) is seen at Romford station having completed its journey from Ilford. (Liam Farrer-Beddall)

Thirty-two Enviro200s arrived between April and June 2011 at Barking, replacing a number of Dennis Dart SLF saloons. 36276 (LX11 AWO) is seen leaving Barking town centre bound for Redbridge on the 366. (Liam Farrer-Beddall)

Catford received a batch of thirteen 8.9-metre Enviro200s in May 2012 for use on route 124. 36529 (LX12 DHJ) is captured by the camera in a wet Eltham town centre. (Liam Farrer-Beddall)

Two months later Bromley took stock of fourteen longer 10.2-metre saloons for route 314. 36549 (LX12 DJZ) is seen heading towards Eltham station, passing through Bromley. (Liam Farrer-Beddall)

It wasn't until June and July 2013 that the next batch of Enviro200s arrived with Stagecoach London. At this time Rainham received a batch of twenty-five 10.8-metre saloons for routes 165 and 256. 36556 (LX13 CYV) is seen in Hornchurch town centre shortly before completing its journey on route 256. (Liam Farrer-Beddall)

In late 2013 Stagecoach London won three Orpington area routes, the R5, R7 and R10, from Metrobus. For this, three 8.9-metre Enviro200s were purchased and allocated to Bromley. 36583 (YX63 LGD) is seen on the R10 in Orpington. (Liam Farrer-Beddall)

Stagecoach was the first London operator to take stock of the Enviro200 MMC model, the first arriving in July 2015. Eight were purchased and allocated to North Street, Romford, for use on the 499. 36601 (YY15 OWU) is seen passing Romford station bound for Gallows Corner Tesco. (Liam Farrer-Beddall)

July 2016 saw the arrival of a thirteen Enviro200 MMCs at Bromley, shared between routes 146 and 336. 36610 (YX16 OHZ) is seen operating route 336, loading at Bromley South. (Liam Farrer-Beddall)

2017 was a busy year for the intake of Enviro200 MMCs with Stagecoach London. The shortest vehicles to be taken into stock measured 9 metres and were allocated to Catford for the 273. 36627 (SN66 WMY) is seen in Lewisham heading towards Petts Wood. (Liam Farrer-Beddall)

Nine Enviro200 MMCs were allocated to Barking for use on the 462. The majority of the batch gained route branding as part of an experiment centred on the Barkingside area of East London. 36636 (SN17 MKZ) is seen in Ilford. Route 167 was also involved in the scheme, with another Enviro200 MMC seen following 36636. (Liam Farrer-Beddall)

36641–69 were delivered to Stagecoach in April 2017 for use on routes 167, 362, 380 and 549. The last four, 36666–9, were longer 10.9-metre saloons, while the others measured 10.5 metres. 36644 (YX17 NXJ) represents this batch and is captured by the camera in Lewisham. (Liam Farrer-Beddall)

Stagecoach London took over operation of the B14 in February 2018 using six 9-metre Enviro200 MMC. The first of the batch 37501 (SN67 WYM) is seen entering Bexleyheath town centre. (Liam Farrer-Beddall)

Twenty-nine Enviro200 MMCs were delivered to Stagecoach London in February 2018. The growth of the company in south-east London saw a new operating base opened at Kangley Bridge Road, Sydenham, this being linked to nearby Catford garage. This became the operating base for 36671–99. The batch could be found operating on several routes into Lewisham, and it is at this location that we find 36683 (YY67 UUD), operating route 284. (Liam Farrer-Beddall)

August 2018 saw seven 9-metre Enviro200 MMCs allocated to Kangley Bridge garage for use on the 356. The last member of the batch, 37513 (YY18 TNV), is seen heading towards Shirley, passing through Penge. (Liam Farrer-Beddall)

September 2018 saw Stagecoach London take over route 193 from Go-Ahead London using a batch of twelve 9.75-metre Enviro200 MMCs. At the same time route 165 at Rainham also gained a batch of longer 10.9-metre, replacing older Enviro200s. North Street, Romford, housed the 193 batch, these being represented by 37517 (YY18 TKE). It is seen passing Romford station bound for County Park Estate. (Liam Farrer-Beddall)

Five Enviro200 MMCEV-bodied BYD D8UR saloons were purchased by Stagecoach London to operate route 323 between Canning Town and Mile End. The last of the batch, 29205 (LF20 XKU), is seen round Canning Town bus station. (Liam Farrer-Beddall)

March 2011 saw London United sold by Transdev to the RATP Group, with Transdev retaining the London Sovereign operation. The new company placed an order for forty-three Enviro200 saloons for use on a number of routes in the Harrow area, and route 251. DE61 (YX11 GBV) was one of those vehicles allocated to Edgware for use on the 251. It is seen entering Edgware station having travelled in from Arnos Grove. (Liam Farrer-Beddall)

When South Mimms-based Sullivan Buses won their first London contract in 2012 they were no stranger to operating the Enviro200, with a number being operated by the company on local services in Hertfordshire and on a shuttle service to Thorpe Park in Surrey. February 2012 saw the company commence operation of route 298. The month before six Enviro200s arrived in an all-red livery. AE14 (KS61 SUL) is seen entering Potters Bar station. (Liam Farrer-Beddall)

Since winning the 298 in 2012, Sullivan Buses have gone from strength to strength, winning three more TfL routes along with a handful of TfL school services in north London. The W9 was, however, the only other TfL service to be operated using Enviro200s. In January 2017 eight Enviro200 MMCs were delivered to the company. AE27 (DB66 SUL) is seen in Southgate operating the W9. (Liam Farrer-Beddall)

Seven Enviro200s were acquired by Arriva the Shires from Arriva London in June 2013. Allocated to Garston, they continued to operate London services, replacing older Dart SLFs and Volvo B6 saloons on TfL work. 3812 (LJ58 AVV) is seen in Harrow operating local area service H18. (Liam Farrer-Beddall)

Tower Transit took over the Lea Interchange, Westbourne Park and Atlas Road garages of First London on 22 June 2013. Eighty-five Enviro200s of varying lengths were acquired by Tower Transit on this date. DML44289 (YX61 FYM) represent this large batch. It is seen passing Homerton Hospital. (Liam Farrer-Beddall)

The first new single-deckers for Tower Transit arrived in February 2015 and were used by the company on route 488 between Dalston Junction and Bromley-by-Bow. DMV45101 (YY64 YKL) is seen parked at the Dalston Junction terminus. (Liam Farrer-Beddall)

Six shorter 9.6-metre Enviro200s were purchased in October 2015 for use on the 339, replacing older Dart SLFs. DM45118 (YX65 RMZ) was one of the batch, all of which were allocated to Lea Interchange. It is seen passing through Mile End on its way to Shadwell. (Liam Farrer-Beddall)

The final new Enviro200s for Tower Transit put in an appearance in November 2015. Three longer 10.8-metre saloons arrived to cover an increase on the 70. The route was later lost to RATP London, and the Enviro200s were redistributed. DMV45114 (YX65 RMO) is seen in Covent Garden operating the now withdrawn RV1 service. (Liam Farrer-Beddall)

Eight Enviro200 saloons were acquired by Tower Transit in October 2019, all originating with First London. The new numbers allocated to them by Tower Transit did not quite match their former identities. DML44182 (YX11 AEW) was new as DML44181, later becoming DE1899 with Metroline. These vehicles were acquired to operate new route 218 between Hammersmith and North Acton. DML44182 is seen passing through Hammersmith town centre. (Liam Farrer-Beddall)

Tellings-Golden Miller won the contract for route E10 in west London in 2014, the route commencing from 31 May. For this nine Enviro200s were purchased by the Arriva Group and based in the Heathrow area. 3430 (YX14 RYV) is seen at journeys end in Ealing Broadway. January 2016 saw control of the route pass to Arriva London. (Liam Farrer-Beddall)

Uno Buses Ltd of Hatfield has an operating area in Hertfordshire, Bedfordshire, Northampton and Milton Keynes, as well as several commercial routes entering north London. In September 2015 the company expanded into London bus operation when, from 25 July, they took over route 383 in the Barnet area. Four Enviro200s were purchased for the route. 602 (YY15 NKC) is seen in Barnet heading towards Woodside Park. (Liam Farrer-Beddall)